happy

by

personogen

seeking with CORE self (BE) – source and derivative
(GEN) – happy

seeking with Derivative self in Action – before and after
(Generator) – happening

seeking with contemplative self (see) – cause and effect
(witness) – happiness

Our Wish for Our Children

We all wish for our children ultimate happiness. We wish for them to have options, flexible choices, freedom to pursue and choose this happiness. All wishes for education are for options, freedom and choice. All wishes for resources are the same. We also wish success in relationships. We wish for relationships where they are appreciated and appreciative. We wish love for them in all its incarnations. We wish passion and connection.

As we lived our lives, we became aware of ourselves in times of freedom and in times of less freedom, or at least we perceived it was less. Perhaps, at our CORE, we always had the same level of freedom. Yet with consequences so clearly in sight, perhaps we chose to believe these freedoms diminished. We stopped looking for what we wanted and started avoiding what we did not want.

The focus away from undesirable is a way to starve ourselves from happiness. Our CORE self, SOURCE of POSSIBLE, operates by direct means. This means we SOURCE a POSSIBLE and it begins to draw into being. Aiming away from possible tends to draw the possible we are attempting to avoid straight towards us. We wish for our children to dream in a way where they seek their happiness without confusion, fear or disintegrating focus on that dream. We wish them clarity, courage and connection.

We wish for them to become aware of who and what they are, so they can SOURCE POSSIBLE and draw it into being, at their CORE(GEN), through their actions (Generator) and by cause and effect(witness). Perhaps

our wish for our children would also be a perfect wish to obtain deep and lasting happiness for ourselves.

There are three kinds of happiness we can pursue. We can pursue happiness in action by making things happen. We can pursue happiness in vision by watching things happen and enjoying the connections that draw and sustain things into being. We can also SOURCE ourselves as naturally happy by pursuing our own depths and allowing ourselves to BE. We are naturally happy at our CORE. We are possibly happy in our derivatives.

Our joy as parents is watching our naturally happy children extend themselves into the world. Some efforts take frustrating practice and puzzling, yet we applaud the attempts that eventually calibrate into success. Our sadness as parents comes from watching our children lose interest in SOURCE of POSSIBLE, dreaming and accepting laws, rules and obligations as a prison of self imposed limits that stops the pursuit of happiness, one avenue at a time until happiness itself eludes them and being naturally happy is something they believe only happens to other people. Some become so removed from their CORE nature of happy that they believe the happiness of others is simply a performance, an act.

While our children remain grounded in their CORE SOURCE of POSSIBLE and learn to reach from naturally happy to happening and happiness, their ability to pursue happiness enfolds for them in a myriad of ways. At first, it appears that they are sustainably happy. Then, on closer examinations, we discover that it isn't that one happiness is sustained, it is more like many small happinesses are SOURCED, enjoyed and realized.

POSSIBLE

How many times have we felt stuck in our lives? How many times have we been stuck in traffic and had a lane open up and the traffic dissolve? How many times have we been confused by a math problem and found the solution and felt our mind stretch in relief? How many times have we felt excluded by a friend and found it was simply a misunderstanding that they felt we were excluding them first? When faced with a circumstance that appears impossible, our world stretches into possible when we SOURCE our GEN and imagine POSSIBLE alternatives, perspectives and actions.

SOURCING POSSIBLE in our CORE aligns us to ourselves and extends a flexible reach from imagining something that makes us happy towards actualizing an action that happens to create happiness. Then all three of our persons share in our CORE state where we are naturally happy. Our Generator makes things happen. Our witness bears witness to happiness.

Isn't happiness just getting what we want?

When many are asked what will make them happy, they state they only want one thing. Then the list grows. As they acquire each thing on their list, their happiness seems abundant. Yet after each thing is acquired, the happiness seems to wane. It is almost as if the process of acquisition makes us more happy than the actual acquisition.

In the dictionary, the word joy is defined as the PROSPECT of getting what we want. This definition seems to shine light on this dynamic. The place between actual acquisition and possible acquisition seems to be highlighted as the kingdom of joy. If you try this with very young children, it is truly fascinating. The child is happy at the suggestion of ice cream. The child is very happy on the journey to ice cream. The child is less happy while eating the ice cream than during the journey to get the ice cream. Then the ice cream is eaten and enjoyed and then the child is still happy, though less happy than when they imagined the ice cream, journeyed to seek the ice cream and experienced the ice cream initially.

What are we to conclude from this? Is it possible that we are more happy seeking than acquiring? Is it possible that seeking is our way to SOURCE our natural state of being happy? How do we seek? How do we SOURCE? How much of seeking begins with conception? How much does focus play into seeking? How much does journey play into seeking? How many kinds of journey are there? Is finding incidental to seeking? Which is more important: seeking or finding? It seems that both are important. Yet finding is the end of the joy that seeking brings. We are natural seekers. From conception of what we wish to seek, to journey of how we will pursue our new proposed happiness to

acquisition, arrival and experience of proposed happiness, our seeker is present in all steps.

Yet finding and acquiring happiness, derived from the journey and acquired SOURCE of POSSIBLE, is less fulfilling than calming ourselves and learning how to simply BE happy. It has often been said that happiness is a choice, a decision. Perhaps the path to happiness has many decisions that make happiness happen. Yet happy has three levels of existence. Happy is in the GEN, BE. Happening is in the Generator's (DO) journey. Happiness is observed and experienced by the witness (see). It is possible to effortlessly BE happy by SOURCE in POSSIBLE. It is possible to become happy in anticipation and action by generating and witnessing emerging happiness.

All three kinds of happiness are distinct. Yet holding an object in our hand will hardly ever provide us with sustainable happiness that we imagine when we set out to acquire the object. Is this because we are ungrateful, unappreciative beings who can never treasure and appreciate what we have? Is this because having is so boring compared to dreaming of having? Is this a "grass is always greener" perspective where we always imagine everything better than it truly is? Or is this dynamic in play because our true nature is the nature of the seeker?

If we are truly, essentially and innately seekers, then our world best serves us as a place of imagining a CORE SOURCE of POSSIBLE, sifting through these POSSIBLES, deciding on one above others, chasing it down and obtaining it. We subdue through seeking. We enjoy through subduing.

Isn't happiness just getting who we want?

Sometimes we seek a connection with a person. This relationship, while we seek it, is enjoyable. When we believe we have acquired the relationship, and thereby association, we have acquired the person, we become bored and seek to seek once more. This leads to restlessness, infidelity, disrespect, objectification, suffocation, disconnection, alienation and loss of the connection. Then the joy of the initial connection is remembered. The connection is craved once more. The pursuit begins. The person is acquired. The person is annoyed at being acquired and attempted to be subdued like a thing. The connection is alienated. The seeker sits back puzzled.

How can I so desperately want something I really do not want? How does a person change so dramatically upon acquisition? How do I find a person capable of sustainable chemistry, connection, and fascination? Do I want a person or do I want a connection with a person?

Ah! When it is stated like that, what does it look like? Instead of acquiring a person, we are acquiring a connection or association with a person. Yet this is still distinct in scope from seeking, acquiring and subduing a thing. A thing can be had and held. A person is innately self sovereign, free. A person is, at their CORE PERSON, a SOURCE of POSSIBLE, vast and infinite within in the scope of infinite possible they can SOURCE.

Then it occurs to us, we cannot acquire a person. Can we acquire a connection? Can we cause a connection? Yet we are already intrinsically and innately connected to all persons at our CORE. So in our SOURCE we are connected. All attempts to describe

10

connections in our constructs and derivatives are less real, less natural than the CORE connection we already have with one another.

It is possible to declare that we belong to another. We are self sovereign and can declare a connection with that sovereignty. We can further declare that we intend to belong with this other through space and time in perpetuity for the duration of this incarnation. In other words, we can decide to stay with one person until death. Yet this decision is not our natural, innate kind of connection. This decision is an artificial, declared connection that must be nurtured, reinforced, enforced and re-decided. Innate connection carries forward through space and time naturally because it is beyond space and time. It exists at our SOURCE, in the GEN.

To experience this innate connection, to realize it, one must SOURCE the POSSIBLE with another. One must realize connection. This connection is not created, caused, activated or found in the before or after. This connection is unveiled as always IS. It is essential in CORE existence, before thought or action. CORE connection exists in the BE. Declared connection exists in the DO. Understood and clarified created connection, found connection, is created as a perspective of the witness.

When connection is innate, it is part of our CORE. It is inalienable. Rejection is impossible. Only declared connection and witnessed connection can be withdrawn and excluded. In the CORE self, connection is constant.

This is why acquiring a person, as if they are a thing, defies their self sovereignty and denies their innate connection to us that has always been. We become

unhappy with a person who owns us, or pretends to own us. We become equally unhappy when we attempt to own a person who may even describe an inalienable and elemental surrender. In truth, their CORE nature is inalienably self sovereign. So while they can share themselves with another through SOURCE of POSSIBLE, their descriptions and decisions to give themselves to another can be repealed and discarded. They have the innate self sovereignty to make it so.

So promises can be discarded. Created agreed upon connections can be discarded. Perceived initial value of another can disappear. All of this confusion comes from attempting to find, cause and create something that can only be realized in our SOURCE.

Lasting connection is SOURCE. It is not found. The kind of seeking that uses the witness to strategize cause and effect, cannot bring lasting connection into our lives. It is not caused. It is not before we seek. It is not after we seek. Lasting connection is a realization of what IS.

Activities that SOURCE the GEN, create a realization of firm and lasting connection. Praise, gratitude, apology, connection, purity, same, happy and possible are GEN SOURCE innate qualities. Praise admires the vast CORE of another with infinite POSSIBLE. Gratitude appreciates the presence and gifts of another's CORE self which stretches our world with POSSIBLE. Apology expresses sorrow in trespass onto the sovereignty of another with clear intent to respect sovereignty in future. Acknowledged CORE connection is a wonderful mystery that we can crave what we

already are so deeply. Purity is our innate natural aligning one to another so we fit perfectly. We are immeasurably and innately SAME. We are innately happy. POSSIBLE is the pool of potential in our GEN.

When a person views another person as a person, they see their CORE first and their Generated and witnessed constructs as incidental. SOURCE of POSSIBLE exists at our CORE. Accessing this SOURCE with another creates sustainable realized connection, connection that always was and ever will be, and IS.

So while momentary happiness may be getting who we want, which a person cannot be acquired in a manner that is real and sustainable, truly being happy comes from SOURCE of POSSIBLE shared with another person. This aligns constructed happiness into CORE happy, which is always real and present and has only to be realized.

Isn't happiness just brain chemistry?

When we are out of balance by our witness and Generator turning away from our GEN, we lose our realization of how we are innately happy at our CORE. When we turn from our CORE, we lose clarity about our SOURCE. Sometimes we can even lose complete awareness of our CORE SELF.

When we turn away from our CORE SELF and forget our CORE SELF, we lose memory of the steps that SOURCE the CORE into our personality, our decisions and our lives. We describe ourselves as merely a visible being. We forget our witness of the disconnection of the decision to attempt to alienate the CORE and MOST HIGH, MOST ORIGINAL SELF.

A child wanted a cookie that the parent wanted to deny the child until after dinner and vegetables were eaten properly to ensure the child's nutrition. The child decides the parent does not truly understand what they need or how much they really need the cookie. The child steals a cookie from the cookie jar and hides it in his room. The parent is cleaning the room and finds the cookie.

The parent asks the child, "Where did you get this cookie?"

The child responds, "It was just there."

"The cookie was always here in your room?"

The child nods.

Now this looks like lying. Yet sometimes we forget things from decisions we have made. The child is mystified by the presence of the cookie. The child has forgotten he hid the cookie. The child has forgotten about the cookie jar altogether.

The parent takes the child back to the cookie jar.

"Did you get this cookie from the cookie jar?" the parent asks.

The child blinks at the cookie jar in surprise. Suddenly the path of the cookie to his room is remembered. The child smiles at the parent. The parent is confused. The child looks unrepentant for stealing the cookie. The child looks surprised when facing the cookie jar. He had forgotten it entirely.

Now the child is growing. The child's parent goes to pick up a child at school. Their orange child is playing with a blue child. The parent tells the child that blue children are bad, dangerous and mean. He tells the child to avoid blue children in future and in fact all blue people. The child returns to school and considers the words of the parent. They play with the blue child anyways. Then one day the blue child accidentally knocks down the orange child's building. The orange child looks at his rubble and remembers what the parent had told him about blue children trying to hurt him. He decides the parent is right. He makes a decision to avoid blue children in future.

Now the orange child is a teenager. He is attracted to a blue girl. He approaches her to talk. He gets angry because he is attracted, yet he has made a decision long ago that all blue people intend him harm. He has

forgotten how he made this decision, yet he carries it forward with him in time, reinforcing this decision with new examples of the injuries by others from blue people.

The blue girl sees him looking at her. She says hello. He responds by saying, "All blue people are bad."

The girl is surprised. She questions him, "Why do you think that blue people are bad?"

"They just are," is his response.

He has turned away from the SOURCE of his decision. He has narrowed his focus over the years to only collect data on how blue people made mistakes or hurt people. He neglected to collect the same data for orange people. He neglected to collect data on blue or orange people that showed how they helped others. So he maintains his decision that blue people are bad, unaware of giving himself the command to only look for bad things from only blue people.

"Orange people are sometimes bad," she tries to understand.

"Blue people are ALWAYS bad," he affirms his narrowed data.

Until the boy widens his perspective to include the activities of all persons and acknowledges that sometimes everyone hurts one another and acknowledges the SAME that we all are at our CORE, he is locked in one dogmatic perspective that limits his life.

What if brain chemistry is the ONLY SOURCE of happiness? Once brain chemistry is balanced and misfortune happens to a person, is the argument going to

attempt to uphold the chemistry perspective as singular, or is the argument going to widen its perspective to include other causes of happiness or other SOURCE? It is possible to argue that once a bad thing happens to someone and they are saddened that their brain chemistry changes. This is true. Yet who decides if something is going to be saddening or uplifting?

Two kids sit in the hallway, happy. They are waiting for their prize for winning the spelling bee. They have tied. The principal comes out into the hallway and hands each of them a chocolate bar. One child loves chocolate and is happy. One child is allergic and is sad. The sad child then considers how much her mother loves chocolate and shifts her perspective from sad to happy. She decided. Both children had brain chemistry that made them predisposed to have the capacity to experience happiness. Yet this happiness can be embraced or denied based on decisions.

Brain chemistry is one thing. A person's choices are something else entirely. Both seem to be essential to happiness. The most balanced brain chemistry in the world can become imbalanced when a person has decided to worry, fear and stress. Similarly, the most imbalanced brain chemistry in the world can be balanced when the person chooses to believe, SOURCE POSSIBLE and have confidence. Does brain chemistry cause happiness? Or does happiness effect brain chemistry?

Mentally Predisposed to Happiness

While unhealthy and imbalanced brain chemistry can undermine happiness, unhealthy and imbalanced decisions in the mind can undermine brain chemistry and ultimately happiness.

Subroutines (Forgotten and Undetected Decisions)

Subroutines are mini programs we have created for ourselves to remind ourselves, protect ourselves and delegate some tasks to a less conscious perspective. These subroutines are awesome if we can remember we are the one who set the subroutine in motion in the first place. If we are conscious of creating the subroutine, we have the power to edit or discard it when its use is no longer applicable or required.

Some subroutines come to attack those we love and even ourselves in an effort to defend ourselves. It is far better to understand our subroutines so we can edit and discard them, rather than alienating others and abusing ourselves for a subroutine that may no longer serve us.

Subroutines are created to remember and act on our behalf. Let us say you are in first grade. There are a bunch of children standing around at lunch. One child says something that hurts another child. You speak up and whip out a real zinging retort that embarrasses the person trying to hurt the child and rescues the hurt child from pain and humiliation. This is all well and good until someone does the same thing to you. Your response to these series of unpleasant interactions is to create a grand rule to never speak around classmates and peers again. At first, you have to concentrate to not speak. Then it becomes an unconscious habit, a subroutine.

Then third grades rolls around. The subroutine to not speak is running quietly in the background. Your teacher offers a prize to the first one to raise their hand to answer a question. In order to answer this question, you have to know the answer AND overcome your previous programming of yourself. So you raise your hand and in

a grand force of will to overcome the prior subroutine you yell at the top of your lungs the answer.

If you were aware of the previous subroutine, you could edit or discard it consciously. Instead you now have a new subroutine. One subroutine commands that you do not speak in front of your peers. Another subroutine requires that you do speak in front of your peers in class. This creates anxiety as you are conflicting with yourself every time you speak in class.

We create millions of these subroutines over our lives to strategize behaviors that will prevent social unease, promote safety, and enhance relationships. The trouble with subroutines is that they often conflict. The other trouble is that they are often poorly tailored to independent and unique circumstances in the future for which they are created.

Conflicting Subroutines

Conflicting subroutines can lead to frozen will, alienation, car accidents and more. If you are pulling into an intersection with a red and a green light displayed next to one another, you are in trouble. One subroutine is telling you to stop at the red light, another subroutine is telling you to go with the green. You are frozen, unable to decide.

One subroutine tells you to protect human life. A circumstance arises where you are put in a position of choosing one human life over another. The subroutine requires that you protect all human life, yet if one human is going to kill another and the only way to stop them is to take their life, can you ever perform this act without incredible inner conflict?

Subroutines help us operate in a relaxed manner in some ways. Yet if we do not have the keys to unlock, edit and potentially discard subroutines that are out of date, or no longer applicable, then we can end up as a ball of conflicting subroutines that are the source of anxiety. We would be at the mercy of our subroutines.

Imprisoned witness

When our mind, our witness, is unaware of itself and its programming, it has very few tools to resolve anxiety, stress and inner conflict. This can lead to strange behavior, paranoia, confusion, alienation of others and more. While our witness is locked out of awareness of the subroutines running and the creation of the subroutine itself, they are imprisoned by the subroutine and at the mercy of its programming.

SOURCING POSSIBLE

When our witness is imprisoned, it freezes our Generator. We can no longer think or act with clarity or elasticity. There are only rigid circles responding to rigid rules. The mind is locked and action cannot be chosen from so much confusion.

When two of our three persons are so incapacitated, it is a clear sign that they have been ignoring the third, MOST HIGH PERSON. It is a sign they have turned away from their SOURCE, their HEART, their CORE.

The Ignored SOURCE

Why do we turn away from our CORE self? It often begins with wanting to ignore the heart to do something the mind prefers. If the heart and mind cannot agree, the mind can turn away from the heart and act on its own. This works for a few moments until the mind needs more POSSIBLE to have an array of choices. Then the mind will choose from choices in the past. It intends to continue to ignore the SOURCE as the SOURCE was judged as imposing.

The Denied SOURCE

Once the SOURCE is ignored, the mind takes further steps to deny the SOURCE ever existed. It proclaims itself as the new MOST HIGH PERSON of ourselves. It erases recorded memories of the SOURCE of its thoughts and Generator's actions. Now when the mind asks itself where an idea came from, it has the experience of the idea always just being there. While it denies the SOURCE, it cannot also acknowledge its contributions.

Seeking SOURCE

When we have ignored, denied and sought to erase all memory of our CORE self from our conscious mind, it is now necessary to seek our CORE self to awaken ourselves to our SOURCE of POSSIBLE. The first step in seeking SOURCE is to ask a question of POSSIBLE.

Is it POSSIBLE that the SOURCE exists?

Now watch your mind imagine. Now watch your mind watch another of yourselves as it sources possible from this SELF. If the mind tries to turn away from the SOURCE again, it will leave a trail back to the SOURCE that disappears into thin air.

That invisible SOURCE is the FIRST person of our PERSONS. It is our HEART. It is the SOURCE of POSSIBLE, immeasurably vast within us. When our mind connects to our GEN, our SOURCE, consciously and often, it will remember the origin of subroutines. It will find the keys to unlock, edit and discard subroutines and become a more conscious co-creator of its programming and deprogramming. The mind will become free.

All From SOURCE

Everything we have ever decided, originated as a possible from our GEN. Our GEN is invisible and double passive. It does not impose possible onto the Generator or witness. The witness must imagine and then conceive POSSIBLE by accessing the GEN. Everything the witness has ever decided has been sourced from the GEN. Everything the Generator has ever done has been sourced from the GEN. This is why the GEN is MOST HIGH, MOST REAL. It is the ORIGIN of all the Generator and witness have thought and done. It is also the ORIGIN of the Generator and witness themselves.

Seeking SOURCE to Seek Anything

If we want anything in this world, or wish to consider what we might want from the vast POSSIBLE that inhabits our CORE self, we have only to imagine, conceive and then imagine and conceive the small steps that draw that imagined thing into being. The SOURCE is the place where everything was before it was conceived or actualized. It is ORIGIN itself.

The Keys to Subroutines at SOURCE

     The SOURCE holds the keys to our subroutines. If we wish to reprogram ourselves to relax tension, reduce anxiety and find peace, the SOURCE is the place to seek. When we access the SOURCE regularly with our witness, we remember how we came to be constructed by ourselves through our decisions, rules, laws and more. When we see that we, in fact, are the author of ourselves, it is quickly imagined how we could also be the editor.

Dissolving Old Subroutines

Old subroutines are quickly discarded when imagined to fall out of existence and melt away. They do come back, quite weaker. Simply visualize them dissolved, falling, fading, shattering, evaporating, going quieter and quieter, being tugged off into space, being weighed out of our mind, through the center of the earth and out into space on the other side. However we imagine their departure, once reinforced, a subroutine will form to keep old subroutines at bay and dissolve them once they attempt to reform and/or reinsert themselves.

Flexible Constructs

Once we hold the keys to our GEN, we have the ability to make rigid constructs in our lives more flexible and free. The rigid rules that came into play from a forced march by an isolated witness, now can find POSSIBLE ways to coexist in fluidity with a myriad of applications and be flexible within special circumstances.

Elastic Perspectives

Similar to our constructs becoming more flexible, our perspectives can also become more elastic. Prejudices dissolve with regular access to the SOURCE of POSSIBLE in the GEN.

Principles in Possible

With regular access to our GEN, rules are often replaced with principles. While rules aim away from what we do not want, principles guide us toward what we do want.

The Quiet Observer

When our witness is balanced with GEN as MOST HIGH, it maintains access to SOURCE of vast POSSIBLE. This keeps it flexible and free. The subroutines are based on principles that guide us towards what we do want. The witness is quiet, observant, imaginative and happy.

The Noisy Observer

When our witness is turned away from its SOURCE of POSSIBLE, life becomes very impossible. It lives in a noising world where its thoughts seek to assert themselves as most important and most high over the witness. Just as the witness sought highest position over the GEN, so every thought, subroutine and contemplation seeks highest position over the witness.

The only path towards freedom from the noise is to simply turn back towards the GEN and imagine it is POSSIBLE to quiet the mind. Imagine the GEN is POSSIBLE and real. Then the witness' choice to ignore the GEN will be remembered and the noise and rebellion will cease.

Once the witness becomes a person that respects the existence, qualities and self sovereignty of other persons, its creations become mini persons that respect the qualities, self sovereignty and peace of the witness. ("mini persons" is discussed in greater detail in book title "Decisions Matter" by Personogen)

Questioning Limitations and Perceived "Impossibles"

Whenever we are faced with something we perceive to be impossible, imagine it is POSSIBLE. Reconnect to your SOURCE of POSSIBLE. Detecting arbitrary limits is a sign that we have turned away from the GEN. Soak the impossible in the GEN. It will quickly dissolve into possible.

The Invisible Heart

Our CORE, is our SOURCE of POSSIBLE. It is the HEART of our being. It is invisible. Our bodies have a physical heart. Yet the HEART of a PERSON is the MOST HIGH PERSON of their three persons. It is their GEN. The CORE SOURCE of ourselves is double passive. It can be sourced and resourced, yet it does not act, impose and think on its own. It extends itself through the other two persons, its Generator to act and its witness to see and think, using these two persons to SOURCE POSSIBLE, SOURCE CONNECTION, SOURCE SELF SOVEREIGNTY or SOURCE any of the innate qualities that comprise the GEN.

We have feelings, yet these feelings are usually the result of repetitive thought. Deep feelings SOURCEd from the GEN are innate qualities.

The Invisible Mind

While our brain is visible, our mind (our witness) is invisible. While our brain has cognitive capacity, our mind has perceptive and imaginative capability. While our brain can perceive through the senses, our mind perceives through observation, screens of prejudice, interpretations, decided connections and more. The physical world that interchanges chemicals is the realm of the brain. The mental world and the decisions, conclusions and relationships decided and perceived is the realm of the mind.

Our mind is one of the persons of our three persons. When it SOURCES the GEN (the first person of our person), the mind is balanced.

The Invisible Strength

Our strength is demonstrated through our actions into the world. Our strength is actualized from our Generator. Our Generator uses the GEN to SOURCE POSSIBLE. It narrows its focus on chosen POSSIBLE and actualizes this POSSIBLE into the world. This will be one step with something small or many small steps for something more complex. The actualized reality in the new world that is derived from POSSIBLE in the GEN is called the Construct.

The Construct is real, yet it is not as real as the SOURCE of the Construct, which is GEN. Reality is defined as that which is neither derivative, nor dependent. This creates shades of reality that extend out from SOURCE, which is most original and most independent, to Derivatives which are derived and dependent to derivatives of derivatives, which are derived further and even more dependent.

Derivatives are still a shade of reality. We can experience them mentally, physically or both, yet they are not as real as their SOURCE, from which they have been conceived and derived and Generated into the world. Our GEN is this SOURCE. It is double passive and cannot act for itself. In this way, it is weakness itself.

The Generator's strength is derived from the weakness of the GEN. When the Generator accesses the GEN to SOURCE POSSIBLE, it fills its strength from a pool of passivity (weakness). The more our Generator resources the GEN, the more our passive self fortifies our active self with POSSIBLE to actualize. Our strength is made perfect (stronger) by SOURCE of POSSIBLE from our weakest, most passive self.

Holding the GEN as MOST HIGH, SOURCE and Original PERSON of all three persons of ourselves, keeps us balanced and free.

weakness

It is fascinating that the weakest, most passive PERSON of our three persons is the SOURCE of every POSSIBLE that exists, is observed and is actualized in our lives. It is ironic. Potential POSSIBLE and actualized possible show themselves as magnetic and dynamic P/persons.

It is further ironic that the quietest PERSON that is MOST HIGH ORIGINAL SELF is often forgotten, ignored and denied to exist at all by the very Generator and witness that it extended itself to become those same Generator and/or witness. How does this happen?

What motivates the witness to deny the contribution and sometimes the very existence of the GEN? What could the witness possibly gain by declaring itself MOST HIGH of the three persons that comprise us? How does this happen?

The Science of Happiness

Science begins with identifying of a pattern or observations. A question arises about the pattern or observation. What is the cause? What is the effect? What other causes could bring this effect? What other effects could come from variations of this cause? The observations often occur within the physical world. The pattern is a perceived connection that is witnessed, decided or both by the person of the Scientist, a person.

There are many causes of happiness. However, to BE intrinsically happy is an ORIGIN state of GEN that simply IS. So while happy is SOURCED, happiness is caused from a SOURCE of POSSIBLE and Generated into present perception. Happiness is ephemeral. Happy is a CORE quality of GEN. So if we want lasting happiness, we need to SOURCE POSSIBLE in the GEN.

Sourcing Happy at Our CORE

We are naturally happy at our CORE. Once we have turned back to the GEN, we become naturally happy once more. While our witness was turned away from the GEN, it sought to acquire happiness with things and people. Having was judged to be the key to happiness.

Once the witness is turned back towards the GEN, being is the SOURCE of POSSIBLE. GEN has the innate quality of happy. Sourcing Happy becomes possible. Once the witness is turned back towards the GEN, it no longer needs to Generate happiness. It simply IS happy.

www.ingramcontent.com/pod-product-compliance
Lightning Source LLC
Chambersburg PA
CBHW050427290526
45786CB00003B/1426